Single Over 50, Finding Love By Faith

My Love Journey

By: Vertis Erkins

Single Over 50, Finding Love By Faith: My Love Journey

Copyright© 2017 by Vertis Erkins

Title ID: 7046224

ISBN-13: 978-1544993164

Unless otherwise indicated, all Scripture quotations are taken from the Holy Bible, New Living Translation, copyright © 1996, 2004, 2007 by Tyndale House Foundation. Used by permission of Tyndale House Publishers, Inc., Carol Stream, Illinois 60188. All rights reserved.

Scripture quotations marked (KJV) are taken from the King James version of the Holy Bible.

Printed in the United States of America.

All rights reserved under International Copyright Law. Contents and/or cover may not be reproduced in whole or in part in any form without the express written consent of the Author and Publisher.

Cover photo by Kelsey Hopkins used by permission.

*The faith of others will increase yours. Keep praying
Love
Lovethe.*

DEDICATION

This book is dedicated to my family who has given me constant encouragement and has always been on my side.

My mentor, who asked me tough questions and pushed me to excel beyond my own conceived limitations.

To my book writing small ministry group who encouraged and cheered for me.

Table of Contents

Chapter 1 The Power of Words	4
Chapter 3: God Turns Situation	9
Chapter 2: Choices	3
Chapter 4: Forgiveness	20
Chapter 5: Suitability	24
Chapter 6: Personality	28
Chapter 7: You Are Good	36
Chapter 8: Confession	44
Chapter 9: Never Say Never	51
Chapter 10: Develop Your Passion	54
Chapter 11: Prayer	56
Chapter 12: Speak The Word	58

Chapter 1

The Power of Words

"Words kill or words give life"

About five years ago, I started writing a series that I called "Now that I'm ready for marriage where is he"? This was my journaling ritual to release my frustration about not being married. I began journaling and quickly lost interest. As I sit here today and think back on those entries, I realized I'm in the same situation. Sill single. Wow! What is going on? I started the woe is me campaign, "What's wrong with me? Why can't I find anyone? Blah, blah and blah."

As I was praying, meditating and going through quiet introspection, I discovered there is nothing wrong with me. There was a season when I was not ready for marriage. Now, I'm in a season where I'm ready to be married. I am trusting and believing God for the right mate. But before I get to that, this is how my story begins.

When I was young, like most little girls, I wanted to be married and have the house with the white picket-fence, the dog and two kids. That was grade school all the way until high school and then something happened. We had the "marriage assignment." For those of you who did not have this project in high school, you were assigned to the opposite sex in your class, pretend to be married, have a baby, and live on a budget. This assignment, originally, was to prepare you for "the real world". I was assigned, in my opinion, the laziest person in the twelfth-grade class. He refused to do the assignment, did not help with the chores, spent the money and did not help with the baby. His reason: He did not want to be tied down and he wasn't into the "marriage thing." So, for my grade sake, I did all the work and the assignments. But when it came time to give our report, he stood up in class and said, "she was too bossy." I was so floored, I popped him right in the middle of class and said, "I'll never get married."

My teacher and the entire class laughed so hard and asked if we were married for real. I stormed to my seat and decided I would pitch the picket fence, the dog, the kids and especially the husband and become a hard-working career woman. I would never have to depend on anyone.

Wow! Those are some strong words. In Proverbs 18:21 it reads:

"Death and life are in the power of the tongue, And those who love it and indulge it will eat its fruit and bear the consequences of their words."

Had I known the power of words like I do now, I would have thought twice before speaking "I'll never get married."

I'm not sure why that experience had such a bad effect on me. I grew up in a loving home, both my parents were present and some of the times my siblings were great. We had our differences, but I had a happy childhood. My parents raised us to be Christians, we grew up learning the word of God and they made certain we had everything we needed. So why did a fake assignment affect me so much?

Today, I cannot not answer that question, but for the rest of my high school days, I was set on becoming a career woman and made sure everyone knew it.

Chapter 2

Choices

"Choices whether good or bad will always have an outcome. Choose wisely."

After that marriage assignment, things at school went back to normal. I got an "A" for my part, just in case you were wondering. I'm not sure if the teacher felt sorry for me or guilty for assigning me that partner. I left that memory behind for it was graduation time and I would be headed off to college to learn how to become a career woman.

Before heading to college, I would spend one more summer vacation with my oldest sister. My oldest sister was married and lived in another state. We would pile up in the family car and head out to see her. There was a family with a young man our age who lived next door to her. I think he was secretly in love with my sister but never showed it. We were always happy to see him. He was like a brother to us and we always had a great visit. Then it happened, we were outside having fun and out of his house walked this totally gorgeous man and I was in love at first sight. Our friend told us it was his older brother coming back to live with them for a while.

Marriage was now back in the picture. In fact, forget about college, I was ready to marry that day. His name was Lee (not his real name of course). Lee was all I could think about for the entire day and finally, the next day, he waved at me. I thought I would faint. Eventually my friend rolled his eyes and dragged me over to meet his brother. He was completing his first year of college and I would be heading off to start my first year of college in a different state so that was that. He asked for my number and we kept in touch all through college.

The love became real and mutual and marriage looked like a possibility. He asked, I said yes and then the career job offer came and I was left with a decision. Can I do both? It's a possibility. But how would this work? He had a career in one state and now I was being offered a career in another state. My parents always taught me that choices whether good or bad will always have an outcome so choose wisely. You don't get to choose the outcome. I chose to accept the job.

Lee encouraged me to go for my dream. We tried to make it work but the distance for us was too much. We mutually parted company and I was now a completely devoted career woman. I know you are screaming, you could have been married! But remember what I stated earlier about the power of words? I spoke, I'll never get married, I want to be a career woman. I made a choice.

Did I have the opportunity for marriage? Yes. I've had a few opportunities but they were not right for me. That could be your situation. You may have had the opportunities, but for some reason, you made a choice. Don't regret or dwell on the choices you've made in the past. Things will and can change for you if you're ready.

Chapter 3

God Turns Situations

"God's love is so strong He forgives and turns our situation around."

As the years went on, I was enjoying my job and having a great life, but in the back of my mind, I had this desire for marriage. I wanted to be married and I was now ready for marriage. Had I spoken death over being married by the words I said back in high school? That was always in the back of my mind. As I continued working and dating, there still was no marriage in sight.

Now I became nervous because I was in my late thirties then early forties with no love in sight. The panic button was hit and the enemy began to fill my head with things like, "What's wrong with you?" "What have you done wrong?" In various conversations, people would ask me, "When are you getting married or why aren't you married?" I began to let those thoughts dominate my mind. I punished myself for no reason.

Again, had I spoke this death of marriage over me? Was I being punished by God? Was this lack of finding a husband following me because of something I said in high school? I was in mental torment.

I began to search scriptures and pray to God for answers. Through His loving ways, He took me to the story of how Peter spoke with his mouth and denied him three times. That account can be found in Luke 22:56-62:

"And a servant-girl, seeing him as he sat in the firelight and looking intently at him, said, "This man was with Him too." But Peter denied it, saying, "Woman, I do not know Him!" A little later someone else saw him and said, "You are one of them too." But Peter said, "Man, I am not!" After about an hour had passed, another man began to insist, "This man was with Him, for he is a Galilean too." But Peter said, "Man, I do not know what you are talking about." Immediately, while he was still speaking, a rooster crowed. The Lord turned and looked at Peter. And Peter remembered the word of the Lord, how He had told him, "Before a rooster crows today, you will deny Me three times." And he went out and wept bitterly [deeply grieved and distressed]."

I can relate to this "wept bitterly" part. However, God told me that even though Peter denied him, he was still accepted, forgiven, loved and placed back into fellowship with God. God's love for us is so strong that even though we misspeak, he forgives and can still turn our situation around.

Read John 21: 15-21 *"So when they had finished breakfast, Jesus said to Simon Peter, "Simon, son of John, do you love Me more than these [others do—with total commitment and devotion]?" He said to Him, "Yes, Lord; You know that I love You [with a deep, personal affection, as for a close friend]." Jesus said to him, "Feed My lambs" Again He said to him a second time, "Simon, son of John, do you love Me [with total commitment and devotion]?*

He said to Him, Yes, Lord; You know that I love You [with a deep, personal affection, as for a close friend]. Jesus said to him, "Shepherd My sheep." He said to him the third time, "Simon, son of John, do you love Me [with a deep, personal affection for Me, as for a close friend]?" Peter was grieved that He asked him the third time, do you [really] love Me [with a deep, personal affection, as for a close friend]? And he said to Him, "Lord, You know everything; You know that I love You [with a deep, personal affection, as for a close friend]." Jesus said to him, "Feed My sheep."

Mark 16:7 "Now go and tell his disciples, including Peter, that Jesus is going ahead of you to Galilee. You will see him there, just as he told you before he died."

Jesus specifically states "including Peter" to show us his love and how He forgave Peter and restored the relationship even though Peter thought he was out.

Like Peter, God's love for us is the motivation for Him to keep or restore us from negative things we've spoken or regretted. If you have ever spoken negative words about marriage or relationships and regret them, don't think there is something wrong with you and are you being punished. Nothing is wrong with you. Don' t think you are out of fellowship with God. God can redeem you from past negative experiences or from negative spoken words. God's love will restore and forgive. Just look what he did for Peter.

After meditating on his story, I knew in my heart all was not lost and I knew God loved me enough to give me the desires of my heart according to Psalm 37:4:

"Take delight in the LORD, and he will give you your heart's desires."

As I was writing this chapter, this is what I heard from God. *He wants to redeem your bad seasons. A new season is here for you so get ready. The best is yet to come.*

Chapter 4

Forgiveness

"God has not dealt with us according to our sins."

God is a God of love and forgiveness. He is not holding a mate back from you because of something you spoke or because you did something wrong. As I stated earlier, I was mentally tormenting myself. I realized I had allowed the devil to trick me into accepting the idea that I will never get married. The enemy will try to keep you condemned. However, Christ has defeated the enemy. Colossians 2:15 (KJV) it states:

"And having spoiled principalities and powers, he made a shew of them openly, triumphing over them in it."

God has exposed the enemy for who he is; for his lies, his deceitfulness.

Jesus defeated him on the cross and forcibly removed him out of our life. We have to stay on watch and not allow him to walk back in our lives, minds or hearts. God is a God of grace and mercy. He is faithful and just to forgive us our sins.

God has not dealt with us according to our sins. That is the old testament. Can you imagine the forgiveness when Jesus came in the new testament? God is not dealing with you with the mindset of "I know what you did". Psalms 103:11-12 states:

"For his unfailing love toward those who fear him is as great as the height of the heavens above the earth. He has

removed our sins as far from us as the east is from the west."

This scripture shows us that just how the distance from heaven and earth is such a great span, that is how much His grace and mercy is for us. His forgiveness towards us is amazing! But, not only does God forgives us, He requires us to forgive others. Letting go of past resentments, past hurts, bad relationships will free you and allow you to open your heart for the right person to come into your life. Most people think yeah, yeah that's the Bible when the conversation of forgiveness comes up. However, people, scientists, and medical professionals believe forgiveness of self and others is essential to physical and emotional health and life.

The Mayo Clinic is recognized as one of the best medical centers in the nation. The Mayo Clinic deals specifically with the health and cures in the areas of diseases and other medical conditions. The Mayo Clinic has a whole web page devoted to forgiveness. Now, if a medical clinic believes forgiveness is essential to physical and emotional health and your conditions are affected by un-forgiveness, then God knew from the beginning of the earth what He was talking about. That's why He is just and faithful to forgive us so quickly. What an amazing God!

Walking in un-forgiveness is not only treacherous to your health, it can block you from receiving all the benefits and promises God has for you.

Chapter 5

Suitability

"Life is not one sided"

Not all is lost when it comes to marriage at any age. As I was dating, some good and some not so good prospects were appearing. I was now trying to mold and figure out how these men could fit into my lifestyle, what did they have to offer me? How did they fit into my life plans and goals? I was looking for a Lee, my first love. I was trying to find that which I let go. Now no one was good enough. He had to be a certain way, dress a certain way, look a certain way.

I had to change my way of thinking and change the way I looked at others.

After all it was Albert Einstein who was credited for saying "the definition of insanity is doing the same thing over and over again and expecting different results." God was teaching me to shift my attitude and my thinking. God and His wisdom walked me through Genesis 2:18 which reads as follows:

"Then the LORD God said, "It is not good for the man to be alone. I will make a helper who is just right for him."

Another version talks about being balanced or being suitable and complementary. One who balances him.

God was teaching me I had to shift my thinking towards being his helper. I was not just to think about how he fits my lifestyle. I had to shift towards being united. Joined together with each other. Not him fitting my mold but us fitting

God's mold together; like-mindedness one purpose, one God. God said a helpmate suitable for him. If we were to do a study of those words, one would find it means a helpmate that is right for him.

I heard someone say, The B-flat key on the piano is not the same as the C, but together they make a harmonious chord. Together they are the right fit. That is what God has intended for us; to make a harmonious chord with our mate if we so choose to have one.

Life is not one sided, meaning what can he do for me? But what can we do for each other? How can we be joined as one or walk in a harmonious chord as we walk out the purpose and plan God has for us? Are you finding that you complement each other or is it all one-sided? I am so grateful and thankful I now am open to give and receive love. To receive the right mate fit for me. It was a matter of shifting and learning to read, hear and understand God's Word. God is so great and gentle when one is attuned to His instructions.

Chapter 6

Personality

"Appreciate Your Personality"

Shifting does not mean changing your personality. As I was learning not to see if a mate would fit my mold, I was also learning I did not have to change my personality. I was discovering, as I was dating, I was trying to change my personality to meet the ways of the other person. God does not want us to change our personality to please or make anyone happy.

Personality, according to one definition is the sum total of the physical, mental, emotional and social characteristics of an individual. This is the real you who God created you to be.

Trying to change your personality to please someone or thinking something is wrong with you only leads to disappointment. I'm not speaking solely about your character.

Your character is your mental and moral qualities and play an important role within our personality.

Our character consists of those things that let us or others know if we are trustworthy, faithful, kind, loving, peaceful, etc. God speaks of character when He talks about the fruit of the Spirit.

I have a story for you. I was dating this gentleman and I was very interested in him. I thought he was handsome, charming, and very smart. However, He had what I would called great character but his personality was very serious. He was pleasant but always serious, void of showing any emotions. My personality is only serious when needed. I love adventure. I can be found riding the highest, fastest roller coaster in the world. I can be found getting up with family at four a.m. headed out driving to Kentucky to hit the 400-mile yard, antique, garage, estate sale every year. I love to read Sherlock Holmes mysteries for fun. He read lab reports for fun. I like adventure. I get the travel bug, throw a dart on a map and book a flight. He was a strategic planner. As you can see, nothing was wrong with either of our personalities. We were total opposites. I know you are going to say opposites attract. I'm here to tell you, not all the time.

Remember we must be fit for each other, suitable like the B-flat and C on the piano. I liked antique shopping and garage sales in my spare time whereas he spent his spare time going to lectures. I was trying to please him by giving up what I love doing and going to all the things he loved; acting serious all the time. I was giving up my personality, I was not being how God created me to be. I thought if I changed, it would get me to the altar. If I asked him to go with me to things It was a look of "you can't be serious" or maybe it was "are you serious?" Either way, it was a serious look.

Appreciate your personality. Do not deny what God has put in you. You may have to adjust your character but God gets glory from your personality. My activities were beneath him to be seen in places like that, at least according to him. I had to be serious like him. I tried but it did not work. I was trying to change my personality to please him. The only good that came out of that relationship were the best naps ever.

Always remember Your personality is your personality. God uniquely created and formed each of us. Psalm 139:14 states:

"Thank you for making me so wonderfully complex! Your workmanship is marvelous—how well I know it."

Never believe you have a bad personality. God knows your frame. Now, we may need to change some things in our character but not our personality. If you are not trustworthy, you steal, lie cheat, play around, have an affair; that is a character issue. We all can do well to have a character check-up every now and then. But your individual fingerprint is from God. He loves you for it because He is your creator. Why would I give that up for a guy who does not appreciate those things? I almost did. Stay true to you.

If you do not stay true to yourself, you begin to make concessions so a person will like you. People will put demands and expectations on your life. If you give in, it can cause you to shift one degree and your whole personality will change. The door has been opened for condemnation, guilt and shame. Condemnation, shame and guilt can destroy your personality.

My Pastor gave an example one Sunday about personality. He said "changing your personality is like going into war with someone else's armor." What a powerful statement. He then took us through the story of David and Goliath. Do you remember the story of David and Goliath? It's a famous Bible story for children and adults. Goliath taunted the children of Israel for a long time and no one was willing to fight him. David, who was just coming to give his brothers food, heard all the commotion and wanted to know why they were not doing anything. You can read the story in I Samuel 17. We know from the story, David volunteered to go. Saul gave David his armor to fight Goliath.

Taking Saul's armor was as if Saul was saying this is what I would wear if I were going to war. This is what I would carry if I were going to war and so forth.

David tried on Saul's personality (armor) but it did not fit him. It was too big, too cumbersome. David could not fight like he wanted to fight or how God was leading him to fight.

We know from the story David had to strip off Saul's personality and go with his own and he was victorious. If David had gone into that war with how someone else told him to go, he would have been destroyed. I would have destroyed myself if I would have taken on someone else's personality just to get married. Remember, you are fearfully and wonderfully made. God knows us. He wants the real you to shine. Your true personality.

Chapter 7

You Are Good

"Don't spend your life trying to regain the past."

God made me good. I was good when he created me. In Genesis 1:31 and I Timothy 4:4 Both state that everything God created is good. Genesis 1:31:

"Then God looked over all he had made, and he saw that it was very good! And evening passed and morning came, marking the sixth day."

I Timothy 4:4

"Since everything God created is good, we should not reject any of it but receive it with thanks."

If God called me good that means I'm good. Now that we know God made us and what He made, He called good. Therefore, you are good, I am good. There are no mistakes on His part. However, most of us have not come into that realization and live a hurting life.

According to *New YouGov* research, seventy-nine percent of people have experienced heartbreak. Heartbreak can be from past hurts, failed relationships, or the loss of a loved one. Some hide it, some express it and some just refuse to deal with the hurt of pain. Are you hurting from a past relationship, shame disgrace or failure? The devil wants to put you in a state of embarrassment. This is especially true if you are over forty or fifty and have never married. He wants you to feel shame by trying to place a bad thought in your head. He will send a well-meaning friend to say negative things about singleness. He will place people around you where you can over hear negative words about you being an "old maid, or being alone. The enemy is trying to make you think you are doing or have done something wrong.

The enemy wants you to believe you have not been forgiven for some past mistake or incident in your life. He will throw all kinds of fiery darts at you to make you feel shame about singleness.

Don't spend your life dwelling on the past nor on the negative things that have occurred in your life. God tells us in John 16:33:

"I have told you all this so that you may have peace in me. Here on earth

you will have many trials and sorrows. But take heart, because I have overcome the world."

Instead of dealing with suppression or trying to compensate with medication, God wants to free you right now. He wants you free so you can move forward and have the wonderful married life you have been dreaming and desiring.

A friend of mine came to me and stated she received a word about a husband and has not seen him. "I've been tithing faithfully," she said. "I've ask the Lord to show me where I need to repent. I attend church faithfully. I have even gone before the courts of heaven to see if the enemy has something against me that is blocking my answer." She was feeling as if her prayers were not heard or she was still in some type of sin.

Maybe you feel as if you will never get married. You've done all the right things and spoken all the correct prayers. Maybe, you feel like the young lady in the movie "Twenty-Seven Dresses." You are always the bridesmaid and never the bride.

Sometimes we walk through a season that looks like the total opposite of what we are believing. It causes us to think or feel we are not in faith or we have some unforgiven sin. The enemy will try to beat you up with this. He will throw those fiery darts at your mind. Don't take those thoughts. Remember David when he was called to be king. He went into a season where he, the supposed king was running from Saul. Total opposite of the word from the Lord. King Saul hated him and tried to kill him.

If you feel like you are in the fourth quarter season of your life, do not despair. The New England Patriots were way behind the Atlanta Falcons until the fourth quarter of the Super Bowl game. In fact, they were behind by 25 points with 2 minutes 12 seconds remaining in the third quarter. All of sudden a breakthrough came forth and they went on to win the Super Bowl in overtime. God can cause a breakthrough for your situation. He promised your latter years will be greater than your former years. God can redeem the time so I encourage you to never say "my clock is ticking, or I'm an old maid."

God can renew everything in your life. If you refer to yourself based on the experiences of the past, you create a stronghold that will block the purpose and promises of God.

I speak breakthrough over your life that strongholds will be demolished over you. Don't Panic. Harness the power of confession, get in the Word and find scripture promises that speak to marriage. Power is released when you speak words of faith not mixed with fear. What words are you speaking out of your mouth? Are you agreeing with others who talk bad about marriage?

Do not let dream suckers steal your desire or dream. Just because a relationship did not work for them, they are putting their fears in you. Get with God and seek Him. He will speak to you and let you know where that mate is located. He will let your mate know how to find you. Meditate on those scriptures. Make declarations, thank God every day for the answer.

Continue to pray. Continue to ask God to daily to show you what you need to see. I encourage you not to give up and keep moving forward. Make sure you have no judgements in your hearts to close your blessings down. God will open things up for you. You will see and it will be marvelous in your sight.

Chapter 8

Confessions

"Speak the Word until you have absolute faith."

Let's talk about confession. It has been said that we must speak life over what we want. As I stated earlier, Proverbs 18:21 reads:

"Life and death are in the power of the tongue."

Everything God created, He spoke it. Look at the first chapter of Genesis. You will find throughout the chapter "And God said…. And it was so." God wants us to call those things that are not as though they were. Romans 4:19:

"As it is written: I have made you a father of many nations. He is our father

in the sight of God, in whom he believed—the God who gives life to the dead and calls into being things that were not."

I'm so grateful and thankful to God. He always puts us back on the right track to get us to our destiny and to get us to the desires of our hearts. It's amazing to me how God teaches. God was teaching me to change my speech. He was teaching me to change the words I was speaking over my life.

Speak scripture over your situation and stand firm. Pray a prayer using scriptures that promises a husband, a wife, or marriage. Pray until you know for certain you believe that prayer.

Here is a test for you. Say out loud, I believe I receive my mate who is right for me. How do you feel?" Was there a sense of sadness, like "oh I hope so." Was there a sick or glad sensation in the pit of your stomach? Did your heart have a tinge of loneliness or were you glad and excited? Sense what your body feels when you make that statement. If you sense some type of anxiety or fear of not having, then keep speaking the scriptures until you have a knowing in your heart that the Word works no matter what the current situation.

God's word is true and have no fear about your age. Have no fear about your 'clock' ticking as some would say. Take no thought about wondering whether marriage will happen or not happen. Speak the word until you have absolute faith and then when you have that knowing in your heart, it's time to pray. In Mark 11:24 we read:

"Therefore I tell you, whatever you ask for in prayer, believe that you have received it, and it will be yours."

Believe you received when you pray. Get into agreement with someone who knows the Word, believes the word and can pray the Word.

Now since you have prayed and you can sense marriage with gladness and happiness, not from a point of lack, it's time to thank God every day. My daily confession is:

I thank you God I have my mate. He is strong in the Lord; a good provider, loves me and is my best friend. I am a helpmate comparable to him. You can make your own confession but make sure it's from the heart and the Word of God.

God Loves us to speak the Word back to him. Isaiah 43:26 KJV says:

"Put me in remembrance: let us plead together: declare thou, that thou mayest be justified."

It is not because God forgot his Word but for us to know and be sure of the promises he made and to know that we are pardoned and justified by His Grace.

The point is to avoid getting into fear and frustration. Don't quit because you confess the Word one day, standing in faith and have yet to see the physical manifestation. Your prayers have been heard. I love the scripture in Daniel 10:12:

Then he said, "Don't be afraid, Daniel. Since the first day you began to pray for understanding and to humble yourself before your God, your request has been heard in heaven. I have come in answer to your prayer."

Have a mindset of great expectation. Expectation is powerful. When you are thankful and in full expectation, you put yourself in a position to receive. In football, when the offensive line gets up to the line of scrimmage, the quarterback expects to receive the ball from the center. The quarterback gets into a position to receive the ball even before he calls out (speaking the word) the play. He does not stand around having idle conversation. He is expecting the ball.

The same is true in baseball. When the catcher crouches down behind the home plate, he is expecting the pitch after giving signals to the pitcher. In this instance, his 'speaking' are the signals given to the pitcher. He then knows what pitch is coming and is prepared. You don't see him preparing to catch the ball by standing up talking to the umpire. God is ready to hike or pitch your blessing to you. Get into a position of expectation.

Chapter 9

Never Say Never

"For Nothing will be impossible with God" (Luke 1:37)."

Wow! You may have thought to yourself, you've done all that and still believing for a husband? Yes I am. Am I worried or panicked about not being married? Absolutely not! I know God's Word is so true and I trust God with every inch of my being. I believe with my whole heart marriage IS. I am in a position of expectation.

It is because of God's love and teaching I am open to love, I am open to give love, and I am open to receive love. I confess the Word and stand on God's promises every day. I speak life over myself, not death. I speak of what God has for me and not focus on what I do not have. I forgive myself, I do not put myself down and know that I am enough. I keep my thoughts and focus on God's Word, I keep negative thoughts away and thank God, every morning for His faithfulness and for my husband.

You too can believe God's promises are true for you. Keep your thoughts and your focus on God and continue to walk with Him and in his presence, nothing is impossible with God. Luke 1:37 says:

"For with God nothing shall be impossible."

What am I doing while I wait? God has given me so many dreams to fulfill and I am having the time of my life getting His purposes done. Fulfilling the plans he has set before me. Writing this book to encourage you. So, we are forty, fifty or even sixty and have never been married. God is a lot of fun. Yes. I'm ready, but until then, I encourage you to fulfill what God has put in you. Go so hard, tears flow out your eyes.

Go ahead and get out of debt. Buy that house. Free yourself up to have time to accomplish the things you dreamed of doing.

Expand your possibility and get creative with the things you want to do. God has a heart for us. He wants you to be happy in other areas of your life. Are you doing the things God spoke to you to do? Has God told you to write that book you've been wanting to write? Go ahead and develop that passion while in your season of waiting.

Chapter 10

Develop Your Passion

"What do you love to do?"

What are you doing with your time? Are you going home from work and spending time in front of the TV? Have you volunteered? Are you working or volunteering in the helps ministry of your church? Are you spending too much time volunteering at church that you forget to do things for yourself? Are you keeping yourself presentable or have you let yourself go? I'm not talking about losing weight, but at your current size now, are you keeping up your appearance?

Learn to recognize God's voice. He will speak to you and tell you to do something or go somewhere. Go! Your husband or wife may be there. Follow the gut feeling which I say is the Holy Spirit prompting you. Do not ignore the Spirit. It may look like you are going in the opposite direction but remember, all the promises of God are yes and to that we say amen.

Ask God to speak to you about your current situation. Have you stepped outside of your comfort zone? There is someone one out there for you. Are you moving when God says to move?

It is time for you to enjoy life and have fun. Don't' be sad and discouraged because of your single state. God wants you to have fun. Stop being a stiff neck people. Literally!

Chapter 11

Prayer

My prayer for you is that no matter your age; no matter that you are thirty, forty or fifty, God will open the windows of heaven blessings over you.

Heavenly Father I pray for my brother or sister right now. Open the eyes of my brother or sister and allow them to see all the glorious things you have prepared for them. Allow them to position themselves to meet the right mate for them. I pray for the anointing of marriage to move forward on their lives. In Jesus name. Amen.

I hope you gained insight into some things you can do to stand strong and change your situation. That's only if you still desire to be married.

Chapter 12

Speak The Word

Please know that with God, all things are possible. Break off the loneliness mindset. Break off the fear of being single. Let go and let God begin to change your heart.

Here are some scriptures to meditate and confess. When you speak these out loud, your faith will rise to new heights in your heart.

Then the LORD God said, "It is not good for the man to be alone. I will make a helper who is just right for him." (Genesis 2:18).

Take delight in the Lord, and he will give you your heart's desires.

Commit everything you do to the Lord. Trust him, and he will help you. (Psalm 37:4-5).

So you also are complete through your union with Christ, who is the head over every ruler and authority. In him lie hidden all the treasures of wisdom and knowledge. (Colossians 2:3, 10).

And if God cares so wonderfully for wildflowers that are here today and thrown into the fire tomorrow, he will certainly care for you. Why do you have so little faith? (Matthew 6:30).

For the Lord God is our sun and our shield. He gives us grace and glory. The Lord will withhold no good thing from those who do what is right. (Psalm 84:11).

Get excited. Some amazing times are headed your way. I believe God is positioning you for the best years of your life.

Write your own confession here:

_____

_____

_____

_____

_____

_____

_____

_____

_____

_____

_____

_____

_____

_____

_____

_____

_____

Carry this with you and speak it every day.

I pray that you were encouraged by my story. Now that you've read this book, if you feel like I've provided you with encouragement and valuable information, would you do me a HUGE favor? I would really appreciate if you would write me a five-star customer review for this book on Amazon. Hopefully, our paths will cross at some point in our lives and we can meet. I would love to hear your journey and rejoice with you over your mate. I pray you will be blessed with a great mate, perfect health, abundant wealth and never ending happiness! God bless!

About the Author

Vertis Erkins, the author of Single over 50, finding love by faith lives in Columbus, Ohio. She is a licensed Realtor® in the state of Ohio. As she walks out her love journey, she encourages and prays with other singles looking for love. If you are single over 50 and walking your own faith journey for finding a soulmate and finding marriage, Vertis will stand in agreement with you as you are believing and trusting God. If you want to be included on her prayer list, send an email to: erkins3@icloud.com.

Made in the USA
San Bernardino, CA
06 May 2017